HEX

Carol Rumens was born in 1944 in South London. A former poetry editor of *Quarto* and *The Literary Review*, and co-editor of *Brangle*, she has won several prizes for her poetry, including the Alice Hunt Bartlett Award, the Cholmondeley Award and the Prudence Farmer Prize. *Star Whisper* was a Poetry Book Society Choice, and she has since received several Poetry Book Society Recommendations and Special Commendations. In 1999, her collection *Holding Pattern* was shortlisted for a Belfast City Arts Award.

Based in Belfast for some years, where she was Poet in Residence at Queen's University, she has also held residencies in Cork, Canterbury and Stockholm. She has been Northern Arts Literary Fellow at Newcastle and Durham, and currently teaches Creative Writing at the University of Wales, Bangor.

Carol Rumens has published eleven books of poetry: *A Strange Girl in Bright Colours* (Quartet, 1973); *Unplayed Music* (1981) and *Star Whisper* (1983) from Secker; *Direct Dialling* (1985), *Selected Poems* (1987) and *From Berlin to Heaven* (1989) from Chatto; *Holding Pattern* (1998) from Blackstaff; and *The Greening of the Snow Beach* (1988), *Thinking of Skins: New & Selected Poems* (1993), *Best China Sky* (1995), *The Miracle Diet*, with cartoons by Viv Quillin (1998), and *Hex* (2002) from Bloodaxe. She has also published a novel, *Plato Park* (Chatto, 1987), and has edited two anthologies, *Making for the Open* (Chatto, 1985) and *New Women Poets* (Bloodaxe Books, 1990) as well as Elizabeth Bartlett's *Two Women Dancing: New & Selected Poems* (Bloodaxe Books, 1995).

Her first play, *Nearly Siberia*, was premièred by the Pascal Theatre Company in 1989, and a new play, *Suzanne Hecabe*, was performed at the Arden School of Theatre, Manchester, in their Festival of New Writing in 2001.

With her partner, Yuri Drobyshev, she is an occasional translator of Russian poetry. Groups of their translations appear in Irina Ratushinskaya's *Pencil Letter* (Bloodaxe Books, 1988) and Evgeny Rein's *Selected Poems* (Bloodaxe Books, 2001). Other poets whose work they have co-translated include Blok and Mandelstam (*The Greening of the Snow Beach*) and Slutsky and Akhmadulina (*Best China Sky*).

Carol Rumens

H E X

BLOODAXE BOOKS

Copyright © Carol Rumens 2002

ISBN: 1 85224 602 2

First published 2002 by
Bloodaxe Books Ltd,
Highgreen,
Tarset,
Northumberland NE48 1RP.

www.bloodaxebooks.com
For further information about Bloodaxe titles
please visit our website or write to
the above address for a catalogue.

Bloodaxe Books Ltd acknowledges
the financial assistance of Northern Arts.

Cover printing by J. Thomson Colour Printers Ltd, Glasgow.

Printed in Great Britain by
Cromwell Press Ltd, Trowbridge, Wiltshire.

For Yura

*To be alive then
was to be aware how necessary
prayer was and impossible.*

R.S. THOMAS, 'A.D.'

Acknowledgements

Acknowledgements are due to the editors of the following publications in which some of these poems first appeared: *A Conversation Piece* (Abbey Press, 2002), *Black Mountain Review, Fortnight, The Irish Review, Last Words* (Picador, 1999), *Metre, Modern Poetry in Translation, Mslexia, Poetry Ireland Review, Poetry Review, Poetry Plus Festival Anthologies, Poetry Scotland, The Rialto, The Review, The Shop* and *Thumbscrew*.

'Shade' was in the Millennium Art & Poetry Exhibition at the Courtauld Gallery, Somerset House in 2000. 'A Rarer Blue' and 'Quotations' were printed in letter and poem-card format respectively by Turret Press. 'Wood Lovers' appears in *An Anthology of Contemporary English Poetry for Russian Readers* (Perspective Publications, Nizhny Novgorod, Russia). 'Kings of the Playground' was a runner-up in the 2001 Cardiff International Poetry Competition, and 'Against Posterity' won first prize in the 'Stay in Touch' section of the National Poetry Competition, 2001.

Contents

9   *The Hex, the Quest...*
11 December Tennis
12 Kings of the Playground
14 Shade
15 Droplets
16 Nadir
17 The Perfect War Machine
18 Rigor Mortis
20 Starlight: A Story
22 The Thingless Phrase
23 Just as in 1914
23 Religious Education
24 Eichmann in Minsk
25 Falling Man
28 An Unsentimental Education
29 The 'Pastime' School of Poets
30 Uxbridge Road: Sex & Charity-Shopping
30 Kitchener Street: Flights of Fancy
31 The Quest, The Hex, The Alkahest
36 Last Minute Gifts
36 The Arrival
37 A Rarer Blue
38 The Submerged Cathedral
40 The Sky and John Constable
41 John Constable and People
42 John Constable and Faith
43 Evolution, 12th September 2001
44 Pietàs
45 Against Posterity
46 Pledge to the Freight Canvasser
47 Anything/Nothing
48 To the Shipbuilder, his Tabernacle
50 Wood Lovers
51 Refresher Course
52 Swedish Exchange
53 Portrait of God as a Creative Writing Student
54 Quotations
55 A Word I Used to Know
56 The Omen Bird
57 The Tour

58   The Polio Cup

60   Mothers/Daughters

60   Learner

61   Letter

62   The Fitting Room

63   Autumn Colours

64   Rogue Translations

68   Genesis: The True Story

69   To the Future Generations

70   When Midnight's an Hour Away: A Pastiche

71   Rich Rhymes for Stroking Small Pets

72   Crazy Jane's Latest Ballad

74   Letters Back

80   The Turnstile

The Hex, the Quest...

Hex has nothing to do with curses. A curse, by nature, is diametrically opposite to a poem. But there are poems here that come out of feeling, sometimes, *as if* hexed. My long-term partner, to whom this book is dedicated, was diagnosed with cancer in 1995. Marvellously, he is alive and cheerful at my side as I write in the summer of 2002. But his condition can't be cured, and it has been very hard to face losing that sweet, 'grow old along with me' kind of future which luckier couples look forward to as they age.

The pains of mortality are universal. However, I also feel, and have felt for several years, as if there were something more sinister in Britain's air. Dismay about our broken-down, shoddy 'enterprise culture' (we who are middle-aged and older remember public services that served the public, in the spirit of *honest* socialism) has been compounded, since September 11th 2001, by a sense that the Western powers are morally out of control.

It's a very long time since my fortunate country was invaded. Yet, if I had to single out one element which has consistently haunted my larger consciousness, it would be war. I grew up under a bomb-damaged roof in south-east London in a household where my parents (both World War I babies) reminisced endlessly with my grandparents about what they called 'The War' (the Second World War). I watched footage of the concentration camps on TV and my faith in God melted amongst the corpses. The Cold War dominated my teens; Vietnam, my early 20s; Northern Ireland, my maturer years. I am naming the few that most impinged – a fraction of those wars and civil wars actually occurring. Now, in my 50s, I wait for another coldish war to be fanned hell-hot – the so-called War on Terrorism. Its propagandists are furiously busy, trying to smother freedom of thought and speech. I want to say, and hope my poems sometimes *do* say, don't sign me up, I'm not part of this. But I am signed up and part of this already.

Perhaps it's because we're in a new century, orphaned from the dear old 20th, whose wicked face was, at least, familiar, that age-old evils look newly repulsive. A palaeontologist would argue that *homo sapiens* has had relatively little time to evolve. But we have had time to split the atom, decode the human genome, etc. No intelligent being on earth today can be in any doubt about the effects of war. How much time do we need, for pity's sake, to get a grip on our instincts, particularly on the aggressive territorialism that creates this horror?

Feigning ignorance, I play, in some of these poems, with notions of design malfunction and even designer malevolence. I'm not saying that I believe in them: I'm saying that there's rather more reason to believe in them than to believe our universe is ordered on principles of divine love.

However, there are many poems here that express my gratefulness for, and pleasure in, the gifts of life, and a lingering, maverick sense of (to borrow Louis MacNeice's inimitable phrase) 'God, or whatever means the Good.' Whatever means the Good, I believe that human beings have to construct it. I hope that *Hex* at least sometimes invokes that possibility.

A note on the typography: some of these poems start their lines with capital letters, others do not. Capitals denote a slightly stronger pause between the lines. I tend to use them in the more metrical poems. Where lines begin in lower-case they run on more swiftly.

December Tennis

Winter's first ice!
Green pavings of it, smashed
and sealed on the little lake. No swans,
mallards, kids – only an old ribbed dustbin
rolled on its side like the park drunk on his seat.

To make you growl
Carol, Carol,
I volunteer a toe
and up comes bold black jack-in-the-box, oh
wicked, delicious, soaking one new Nike.

We're for the courts.
Is it Lux or Dreft
they're powdered with? Such velvet
beneath our heels of sky!

Play is the rosebud gift
we gather yet.
Our old wood low-tech racquets
can flash, trampoline, taking
bows when we're in our stride – although
my first shot slugs the net – too low.

There's a circle in Hell
for love like ours. But the ball
survives the serve, the beautiful curve of our planet
reels from our palms, and the sun,
a toe-dipping god, is splashing the trees and the fence
across our dance in huge harmless meshed
Xs and Ys!

Kings of the Playground

All to get the Bully – who hid in a steel-clad cupboard –
the Bully Bashers stormed the trembling school.
They bullied the Bully's kit, his grubby blazer,
his sports-bag, his bully-beef flavour crisps.

They bullied the kids with the bruises
that showed the Bully's shoe-print.
They bullied the gerbils he'd teased, they bullied every computer
he'd slimed with his bully virus.

They bullied the prefects and teachers –
the nice ones first, then the bullies.
The kids who had conduct stars, the kids in detention, even
the football team, they bullied, yelling 'Ya bullying fairies!'

They bullied the books, though the Bully didn't like books:
they bullied the white-boards and black-boards,
they bullied the wall-charts, the registers, the sick-notes,
the pass-notes. They bullied the two- times table.

Then they thundered out and bullied the empty playground,
they bullied the big round sky that covered the playground,
they bullied the rain, the bushes, the used needles,
the trembling waiting parents, the tiny brothers and sisters.

Bully TV was launched. There was only one programme
'How We Bashed the Bully'. Anyone who switched off
was sentenced to 25 years community-bullying.
The Bully-Bashers relaxed. Gave themselves medals. Flew home.

The Bully listened a while, and grinned in the dark cupboard.
He combed his hair. He opened the door wide.
He sauntered through the wrecked assembly hall.
Scared faces turned. Eyes that remembered his bruises

clouded over, younger eyes grew shiny.
Suddenly someone shouted, 'Look, the Bully!
Them liars didn't get him! Three cheers for our Bully!'
And everyone yelled and stamped: 'Three cheers for old Bully!'

Old Bully mounted the stage. How tall he was,
what a lovely speech he made. The big boys lifted him high
and they all stormed into the trembling streets, yelling
'Make way for Old Bully, ya cunts!' And the people did.

Shade

might seem pure negative. But do you remember
when it was solid, delicious as a late breakfast?
We'd been in the fields since 6 a.m., training
the new kiwi-plants to weave thick cool tunnels
for next season's pickers, stringing the wayward tendrils
to the trellises that would lead them up and over.
There were few leaves on those apprentice vines,
nothing to beat back the power of the sky.
We watched our forearms shrivel like eggs in a pan.
What amateurs of the sun, what holy fools
we were, out there in the desert in our tee-shirts,
as if a god would pity human skin.

At noon the day was over, called off.
We crossed the fields to the avocado orchards
where we flung ourselves down, the team of us, speechless.
The cool-box broached, we dived into whole grapefruit.
Can you remember what the word *shade* meant there?
How we pulled it on, over our scalps and eyes,
and it was the end of all headaches?
How we rinsed our faces in it again and again?
How we buried ourselves in its arms and heard our names?
If death were to be like this, would we call it loss?
We'd know, long before we were cold, that a great wish had been
      granted.

Droplets

Tiniest somersaulter
through unroofed centuries,
puzzling your hooped knees
as you helter-skelter,
dreamy, careless,
without a safety net
into an almost-ness
as uneventfully lost,
your house re-let,
guiltless defaulter:

sex: un-noted: weight:
a minimal gravity:
whatever you'd have tried
in time amounting to,
unguessed, undone –
I'd have your cry
brought home – and yet
when you demand to live,
these hands that blessed
your hopeful forehead, answer
only in negative.

Nadir

Then the last luminaries went underground.
The sea expressed its characteristic view
With sighs, and raked harsh echoes from the strand.
Someone pressed at the window to remark
Spring's whitewash on the shit-house good as new.
There was smoke but no fire: there was almost no smoke,
But these would later come into their own,
The luminaries said. As sure as corn
In August, as the rising of the lark,
They'd wet the baby's head, declare it sound
And send it on, green-lit, to Tyrone.

The Perfect War Machine

They fall into line without question and thunder home,
   White as a childhood of happiness, pelting head-on,
Spit-stringy muzzles in wreathings of mane and steam.
   But *is* it happiness, whipping these gallopers home,
Reigning them in, colliding them, laying them down
   Suddenly meek on the shore (which also once leapt in the sun),
The strong white bodies dissolved to a few grey blisters of foam?

And now come the reinforcements, another disciplined team
   Over the top in a tumult of energies.
Happy? Of course. They run with the herd, and every herd is the same
   As far as they know. This lack of significance frees,
Surely, the blind white horses, who gallop and die with abandon,
   Having no myth of themselves, and no desire but the sea's?

Rigor Mortis

Someone should tell them they're dead.
Two rigid soldiers
are facing across a bridge,
facing at point-blank range:

two rigid soldiers,
both men ready to fire,
facing at point-blank range
the shot that stops the war,

both men ready to fire,
when the starter signals,
the shot that stops the war
of two land-eating lands.

When the starter signals,
watched by the empty children
of two land-eating lands,
they fire at each other's frowns.

Watched by the empty children
at either end of the bridge,
they fire at each other's frowns,
two soldiers, sights re-focused

at either end of the bridge.
It's like science fiction:
two soldiers, sights re-focused,
swallowing shot like bread.

It's like science fiction.
This can't be ordinary flesh
swallowing shot like bread,
and poised to fire again.

This can't be ordinary flesh,
its weaponry always loaded
and poised to fire again.
Two bundles of riddled land

in a carcass of battle-dress
are facing across a bridge
they think is worth dying for.
Someone should tell them they're dead.

Starlight: A Story

When we abolished nightfall from our cities
stars by thousands died. Died like the small change
in the pocket-linings of a lottery winner,
or like the secrets of a world language.

Never again would couples, naked-eyed,
point to the true fidelities, dividing
into the one who sees, the 'nil' or 'plus'
dioptric millionaire, and the one who skims a wish-spoon

through inner space and smiles, 'Oh yes I see.'
And yet our easy neighbour went on rising;
the massive dishes murmured. Stars weren't apes or coral
(we blushed), but where we'd left the future niche-less,

north and far west, they peeped through the FOR SALE boards
and swam the flooded fields. Imagine it,
a land so old the only animals,
the only birds, were stars! 'Back', we cried, 'Back to the starlight.'

We made them ours, quick as the half-farmed acres.
We didn't ask, they burst out of the foaming
tantalus of that clear, black, country sky
into our mouths, eyes, hair, mineral as raindrops:

copper, quartz, sapphire, marquesite,
brown diamonds, white. *Not in lone splendour*, no. We dipped
into the bubbling universe of memory
to name the striding lovesick giant, the bears, the twins, the huntress.

Some of us found our god-folk, some, our folk gods:
all the tutelary spirits of our sight
embraced us now we'd dumped the grid to mine
our little clinkable purse of sixpenny physics.

We'd seen the light. And then we saw the dark,
and how it wasn't to be brushed aside
as backdrop to the true show. It expanded,
it gathered speed, rolled in like loosened mountains –

impacted, dayless night. We watered down to shadows.
We were the planet's after-life, its memory
of dark-adapted eyes and hunting glamour,
alerted, impotent. We snapped our press-stud torches

to spots of frost and listened, saw new species
muscling between the trees, and sighed for the slip-roads,
while stars went on being stars, pure brilliance,
of course, but selfish, worse than genius.

Starlight. This, we've learned, was our illusion,
oxymoronic, untranslatable
into our puddled tracks and inked-out signposts. *Starlight*
that dies before it touches us, like love.

We swear – *de mortuis nil nisi bonum*
but each of us has stroked the reeds, confiding
to their long mouths that the dead have cheated us.
We pray, but I believe our prayers have changed

as prayers do change when a life-or-death desire
no longer knocks us out, jetting like water-cannon,
no longer knocks at all, and we drop into our place
at the key-holes of the earth. We are a solar people,

clichéd through with the flash of one near star.
These were our darlings all along: the rock-throwers,
particle breeders, sperm-merchants, suns.
To every brightness its reflective pattern,

and sight, perhaps, but not within our time-scale,
our curvature. To us, the low horizon,
the soiled cloud where we look round for our neighbour.
When the world tilts a little to the right

we say – or is it to the left – we'll see her,
luminous, unoffended, on our wave-length
still – the only one we touched and did not haunt.
'The moon,' we sigh, 'What happened to old moon-rise?'

The Thingless Phrase

(to Edward Thomas, after reading 'The Word')

Though I'm not sure if I could recognise
The voice from that of any song-rich bird,
Now you've marked for me something audible
As *pure thrush word*,
I wouldn't need to hear it twice,
I think, to trace the call
Out of that moment of parenthesis
(Not tuneful, *tart*; translatable to nothing
But un-romantic thrushness):
And if I never have the luck to hear
A thrush text-messaging,
It won't be lost, the mystery of your *thingless*
Name – I'll just keep coming back to where
The poem hears it, and wait there.

BLOODAXE BOOKS

HIGHGREEN, TARSET, NORTHUMBERLAND NE48 1RP

TELEPHONE: 01434-240500   FAX: 01434-240505

E-MAIL: bloodaxepublicity@yahoo.co.uk

Please find enclosed a review / complimentary copy of

Carol Rumens: *Hex*

Publication date: Thursday 31 October 2002

£7.95 paperback   80 pp   ISBN: 1 85224 602 2

FOR FURTHER INFORMATION PLEASE CONTACT CHRISTINE MACGREGOR AT BLOODAXE

We would appreciate a copy of any review or mention you might give this book.

Just as in 1914

You can sell the young
A spell, a pill, a look, a grudge, a land,
Life insurance, God, a band,
A pup, a truth, their youth.

You can sell the young
Girl her own white unicorn.
You can sell the young
Man his own shite uniform.

Name it 'gallantry' or 'martyrdom',
You can sell it. You can sell the young.

Religious Education

The god of human love was king of kings,
Then, to our wooden classroom: where a child's
Finger moved, a small star cruised above it,
Nervously eyeing shapes beyond the wind.
I could dim any light and see it now,
The silver-on-black word, *epiphany*,
And find, brimming my hands, the charged rewards
For having, being, nothing. Is there mercy
In any universe for us, who knelt
Crownless among the hungry, kicking lambs,
And touched the star, we numerous underlings
Who now believe in all kinds of imaginary things?

Eichmann in Minsk

*As I arrived I saw a Jewish woman with a small child in her arms
in the pit. I wanted to pull the child out, but then the bullet hit
the child's head. I got back into the car. 'Berlin,' I said to my driver.
I drank Schnapps as if it was water. I had to dull my brain.'*
THE DIARIES OF ADOLF EICHMANN

Drinking Schnapps like water, stare
Until the moment's hardly there,
Until the shapes in the forest's floor
Stiffen, fade and rise no more
As limbs and mouths with claims to air,

And trees fly back to the clearing where
The bony-shouldered spades prepare
To meet the load from the lorry door,
On schedule, as you'd planned before
Drinking Schnapps like water.

Nothing's there! So grown-ups swear.
So history lies. So bodies bear
The heavy measures ordered for
Disposal. It is only your
Child you pity, almost spare,
   Drinking Schnapps like water.

24

Falling Man

From another angle,
it's as if the lens
had caught him asleep,
dawn-lit, gripped
by one of those vivid
pre-waking bad
dreams, where the brain
e-mails itself:
this isn't happening.
Not the illusion
of stillness, but
the lack of distortion,
casualness, almost,
in his posture, his body's
so-far unflawed
completeness, muddles
our narrative grasp.
He can handle this.
It's only air,
air that was always
our element, made
to breathe and burn,
to be built into,
and risen above,
the trespass-inviting
pitch whose one
amazing floodlight
names us co-stars.

We had to look up:
we bathed our eyes
in light so they learned
colour, stretched arms
and lungs into Os
of desire: we found
trees to feed us,
mountains to teach us,
like sleepers waking,
kept ascending,
poised on the tip

of our soaring backbone
until there was less
and less air: maladapted,
enchanted, we still
saw ways to increase
height, flung up towers,
flew fortresses, looped
skyway to skyway:
we 'conquered space'
as we phrased it, trawling
our own supplies
of oxygen, rushed
up, floated down,
not quite admitting
what thrust had been required,
suspecting we'd grown
at least one small wing.

But the love of surface
stuck to our soles.
And our sun-gods, turning
to stone, sang out
from their beautiful hardness:
dive, plunge,
be scattered over
your disputed cities
and shine beyond memory!
Gods need our trust:
then they'll catch the shadow
of a man, falling,
or a man, flying
into his future,
who smiles as it stops
and spins him a tunnel
in which he hags
as others are hanging
outside their windows
and walls like pupas
waiting to split
into moths, new man-moths,
and fly away, lighter
than poetry.

26

The steeper the fall,
the wilder the angle
of rebound: this
is emotional physics.
We sting as we die,
like ants, we roll
our alchemical dead
into thunderheads, gather
as balled-up stars
and pelt the world
with skull-bits, billions
of crumbled backbones
to feed the soil,
to grow the new tall.
From the air, nothing hurts.
The air itself
is nursery blue
and safe as steel-
threaded towers. And our hands
move over the face
of the deep, they are all-
powerful: look,
they can dump fire
on selected targets
while turning a page
horizontally,
to pause this diver,
laying him safely
on Slumberland foam,
him and his heart-plunging
nightmare, his billowing
shirt, his scream
fading to daybreak's
patter of shower-tiles,
running-shoes, pavement –
the usual welcome
of nearby earth,
G-forces impalpable
now to one quick,
finely-braced ankle,
one kicked-back heel.

An Unsentimental Education

Now it is settling down, the scream.
ELIZABETH BISHOP

When the room toppled slowly round that cry
Your narrowed gaze went sightseeing. Perhaps
Sleep would fall on the effervescent air
If you were kind and studied all the gaps
And quirks in things, exchanged a cheerful sigh
With the white paint-crumb in a portrait's eye,
And tamed with tea those mild ambiguous cups
Whose peep-holes, grains of rice, 'weren't really there'.

In time, you found the sanest point of feeling –
The earthquake zone. A shock-absorbent ceiling,
Slide-away walls in natural-seeming blue,
Turned into planes, boats, buses, with their stock
Of very proper windows. Dared to look,
You'd see the poems, waving hard at you.

The 'Pastime' School of Poets

Poems I might have written for my father,
had he lived long enough, had I learned quicker
to find the vital signs inside the daft
corseted minuets and crumbly sword-play
of borrowed language: had I not ranged against him
my revolution, where a poem was measured
beside the shapes of things just made, lit blocks
I loved, wrought in Black Mountain foundries or
night-brilliant power stations in the depths
of Europe – poems my father couldn't see
at all, and wouldn't touch because they'd burn
harsh chemical shadows, blanching rays
into the poems he loved, the lines he whispered
to make them breathe and enter, turn, and echo
through courteous archways, genuflecting slightly
towards that dangerous place, the margin: poems,
once gifts, now telling him he had no gift,
a man who scribbled 'poems' as a pastime,
a man who *scribbled*: – poems he crushed in bins
or ashtrays, draw their smoke, flatten their crinkled
surfaces and flow across my keyboard
as poems I might have written for my father
for him to love, and to be loved by others;
I stand back as they pass, admiring how
simply they press towards their vanished moment,
freed from gentility, made truthful by
the silence darkening round them, as I once
darkened my poor father with my silence:
poems too late for giving, poems that whisper
if poems don't hurt us, are they truly poems?
but claim no power to burn, are almost weightless
among the graves of books and revolutions
and old beliefs that such things are immortal:
poems I'll write for no one, for a pastime.

Uxbridge Road: Sex & Charity-Shopping

Don't think, because we're poor, we don't touch dreams
When we tweak cuffs and spin the rainbow rail:
We know the stars are moved by colour-schemes.
Don't think we're merely taking cover. Style
Just named its price – or these are not my jeans –
Leather-look retro, darling, not has-beens.
Ask anyone, the winos, the old biddies,
Our one-pound coins buy love, like everybody's.

Kitchener Street: Flights of Fancy

I want you to be real again, bluebird.
If these villagers can grow palms
And pinwheels, father forty moss-cheeked gnomes
And paint girls' names on side-walls, can't you quietly
Take a moment, skim my red-brick rhymes,
Lately so back-to-back, and be the new word
Granted only when sex is taken lightly?

30

The Quest, The Hex, The Alkahest

Hate – what a whirlwind ride
from love to there:

star into black hole, white-hot Mr Hyde
into flaky Jekyll –

believe me, this
wasn't like turning a coin.

It was radical re-design.
So I gathered glass blackberries

from the only rose too wise
to wear fancy suits –

the *alchemilla vulgaris*
and revised my solvents and solutes.

I'd been chucked out of O Level
Chemistry (Cookery, too)

but I knew how to blacken a name,
cure desire and divine the healing kiss

sent in a bubonic bubble
of spit: if love was shit, whatever else

would be no syllogistical trouble.
I turned up the flame, threw in

a flash of salt: as soon as my world of dew
rose to the boil,

I added the can of worms, the tin of stew:
the love-thing. Oh, it glowed

deeper the longer it rode,
slow-tanning to a hepatitis shade

in an ooze of gas on the hollow
crux of each second-hand ring

I rented as I travelled.
I knew I was chemical king of the rolling road

when water was just a ghost
on a distant cheekbone (whose

I didn't care – not mine
any more, ever, amen)

and I stroked its face as the matter cooled
and I called it *the most*

*malleable and ductile
metal*, miraculous *gulth*,

glitter of wealth in the froth
of my gullible self –

no, wait. I was better than that.
I called it hate.

I'd lost my sense of shame.
Soft parts are first to get fucked

as that Hazchem Eucharist
rinses your mind, but

it's the bargain you strike
for the twenty-two carat product.

I played with the target, zapped
some shy peripheral *putti*

(split-splat) then aimed point-blank
at the former seraph –

you. I wanted blood and tears, no pity,
so here was the set-up:

your favourites walked the plank
in front of you. I had you hexed,

hoaxed, on fire, hung from a spike,
gnawed out by cancers,

wild-eyed with Alzheimer's,
laid low by machete attack.

Blood? *It* was only ketchup,
the *kitsch* of the poor, the *kvetch* of the hated

bouncing back, twisting the tale
begun with your very own knife-

thrust through my hero's life: reversal,
darling, the oldest trick:

revenge, if you like. Now, though,
it had your sheen, your brow:

it would last forever, my septic
passion, tender and true

as erectile tissue,
secreting radiant ink

like the real thing. Not so.
Think, if you dare,

how the dead live. A new
corpse is a gas,

all go in its green-blue-pink
bio-bright kit, it dances

a day or two, yes,
then slithers off back to bed, lies down

abandoned, random, done.
when the last degradable bit

has gone, the glamour has.
And hate's like that.

Dead love is jazz. Dead hate is zilch,
zero, the emptiest flat

in the writer's block, the binned obit.
It's a legless bug, a glugless sink:

it's darkness visible –
but you need to be Milton to see it.

After a final belch
at the dizzy alchemist

to deliver a knock-out hit
of isopropyl methyl-

phosphorofluoridate,
it pisses off to wherever

Stork lies down with butter.
And maybe, somewhere, the difference doesn't matter:

Base and Precious wed in a silvery mist
on an aisle in some Tescos

for stars – that's Chemistry
for girls. But Alchemy? Sheer spin

and greed, like the other thing
which makes the world go round

the twist and reappear
decidedly pear-shaped.

Don't think I'm being moral:
given a local fount

of elixir, a pinch of salt,
a body that seemed to count,

I'd kill tomorrow.
But no one's there. Or here.

Hyde snuggled back inside
Jekyll (*Look, no hair*).

Dew's dew. My rose, you
aren't much of a rose

since the alkahest jumped cup.
Tin of course continues

to be tin: functional, cold,
often found empty. Gold? We made it up.

Last Minute Gifts

A cool Talk Pen (*record and play back your own message*),
one litre of ten-year-old Laphroaig, some Re-Vit Body Massage,
a sweater-bear, three hundred grams of Continental Truffles,
a box of Lancome's *Coleurs*, plus a few other cosmetic trifles,
were found untouched in a Duty Free bag in the dead woman's home,
like chromosomes that had never mated, planes that had almost flown.

The Arrival

There are days early in love when love knows nothing
but to exist between our thoughts, unremarkable, vaguely
grand – as the future did when we were children.
Nothing becomes love more than when he dozes
like this, a jet-lagged wanderer, curled over his wallet,
his possibly false papers. *I'm the one:*
arrest me! is the last thing he would say.

A Rarer Blue

Bluebells were once as common a surprise
for a London child as the sea. I used to cherish
their tiny pinstripe, curly nostril-whiskers.
How they'd make a whole wood wade in blue
interested me less than the shameless juices
webbing my hands, the questions of collection:
how many bunches to a vase, why death
had sealed so tight the newest topmost bells.

Now, it's always the wrong wood or season,
their ghosts a spiky reticence
and, any way, forbidden.
Now I would like to see the matter dropped
in a sadly unenlightened childhood
and give my gaze to the heath-dwelling solitary
who lets the island shine through all her panes.
She likes a northern coast, but she isn't snobbish;
she gleams on Sussex, too, my wakeful lantern,
eye of the grass, mouth of the dawn, stone's sea-glimpse –
the little shaken harebell that won't be pulled.

The Submerged Cathedral

(in memory of Phyllis Robinson)

> *I have made mysterious nature my religion…to feel the*
> *supreme and moving beauty of the spectacle to which Nature*
> *invites her ephemeral guests, that is what I call prayer.*
>
> CLAUDE DEBUSSY

It's an hour before the dawn of rock 'n' roll:
Music has not so far been made flesh –
Or not for a working-class girl of thirteen.
And then I watch you play, star graduate
Of James Ching and the Matthay School,
Your technique so physical, so lavish,
I'd call it, now, *l'écriture féminine*
For pianists: but in 1958
All I know is that you are what you're playing –
You're playing *La Cathédrale Engloutie.*

A camera's drawn to the concert pianist's hands,
Caressing octaves, palely capering –
Sunday *Palladium* stuff, with Russ Conway
Or Winifred Atwell (coos from the mums and dads),
To be filed under my new word: *Philistine.*
This is art so deep it's industry:
Music as white-water, which your spine
Channels, springing arms transform. That's how
You lift and tumble these ton-weights of bell power:
I watch you, not your hands. I watch the sea,

Out of my depth, though, like *La Cathédrale.*
I mean all this to last – the eight hours' practice
Each day, hopeless devotion – and it does –
In other contexts. Oh, I bury it,
Music, and you, and all the pain of childhood,
But lumber back like a mediaeval builder
With washed-up stones (some good stone, too) and prayers,
To raise another heaven-touching marvel
On the same flood-site, watch another tide
Swagger in and demolish every bit.

38

After the last wreck, when I'd declared
The end of building-works on any coast,
Strange bells began to ring for me, the tone
Rubbed ordinary by forty years, but true:
Ghostly but not damned. What if the ghost
Wryly sang, 'Promises, promises?'
It was a gentle challenge, after all.
The sacred stones were myth. The tide that reared
So vengefully, hauled by the same moon,
Was myth. Not so, my common ground with you.

How we talk up 'the generation gap',
Break our necks in it, and never find
The friendly criss-cross trails of co-existence –
That gift which is to pause at one epoch,
The people of one earth. Yes, the years wear us...
But may all years be worn as you wore yours
That day we met, with teacherly compassion,
Because the body knows when the brighter mind
Rejects it, sulks like an untuned piano:
You lived in yours (it knew) like the luckiest girls.

It's hard, though, for the tired cells to sightread
Their last prélude, fingers twisting palm-ward,
In search of rarer ivory, their guiding
Beat a laggard stone-deaf walking-stick.
Like Schubert's songs, off in another key
Before we can say 'swan', you were elsewhere:
And elsewhere, in a room nearby, your music.
I'd wanted you to play. I let that go.
You counted off your new pursuits, confiding
'I love the sea. I love to watch *la mer*!'

On Portrush Strand I watch it too, engrossed
Like a child beside a piano, half aware
That this, whatever 'this' may be, won't keep,
The waves themselves won't keep. But someone plays
Debussy. Something drives the bright white horses
You're not admiring now – not from these shores,
And makes them flesh, as music was, for me,
An hour before the dawn of rock 'n' roll
When you, star graduate of the Matthay school,
Lifted the great bells out of the sea.

The Sky and John Constable

Portray the artist
   As justice:
In his scale-pans,
   Foreground and background.
He places an ounce-weight
   On foreground, adds another:
Tall background rises
   Like grief into his eyes
   And can't be wiped.

A widower has no hunger
   Except to paint
Sky, sky as it should be –
   Enormous dynamo
Of *brilliancy and consequence.*
   No cornered afterthought
Will not return its power
   Via the wisp of a mill-sail,
   A gilding of wheat.

How can bodies, food
   Exist in the light of death?
But he is entrusted with light:
   He is the artist. So
Portray him as division
   Between his torn sky
And his worked meadows,
   The perfect ounce of justice
   Weighing on him:

   Weighing his lightness.

John Constable and People

1

How many strokes to a hireling
  Compared to rich pasture?
He is an item, eloquent
  Only in gesture.
He never stops and stares,
  Being a nobody,
A loose hair on the sleeve
  Of things, a streak of texture.

But this is his gallery.
  He directs the vast
Herdscape of hills,
  Sculpts in mud and grazing.
He himself is grass,
  His only resurrection
Through steam and fire towards
  The frame. The funerals.

2

A boy too heavily scolded
  Dips his face to the beck
And tells it everything.
  He is not of the elect,
This portrait-hater.
  Though he'll yearn to please,
He'll not be watering down
  His clouds, his candour.

One day, when he looks up
  He'll see miles past his thumb:
There stands the rarest cloud,
  Its human features forming
Ringlets, necklace, snow-
  Fall of her Empire-line,
And, at the vanishing point
  Of generous laughter, him.

John Constable and Faith

He says: 'These pictures are experiments'
and he finds out how the cloud-shadow touches
the mill-stream, records its altered volume.
He plots effect to cause, measures the lean
of a rotted post, the sinkage of a cart-wheel.
But when the earth can't wait for Easter Sunday,
when the little starry blizzards
are whirling out of every finger of blackthorn,
there's nothing to test, to doubt, in the stun of that cry:
'I am the Resurrection and the Life.'

This is not how we do science, not what nature tells us,
speaking out of the slowing heart of summer,
the sharpest claws alert for what they can seize
in the fields we never paint any more, as in the desert cities
whose burning we will photograph tomorrow.

Is it knowledge, or some quick brush-stroke of faith
binds us to him still? We can't unweave them.
But if he says his clouds explain the velocity
of heaven's breath, we stare, and lower our voices,
as if we hoped to hear some new announcement,
or the old one, making sense in a new way.

Evolution, 12th September 2001

Some mornings, light is hard as the grassless mountains
and mis-timed adolescence breaks out in my bones.
When I try to look up, eye-remnants, fragments of chitin,
swirl and crackle together, aspire to a brain.
I have evolved into something that shouldn't exist,
optimal, powerless, hatched in the wrong house.
They've furnished it horribly: the hardwood frames
are prison surplus. When I buffet the glass
it stuns me like the language-user's lies.
I shall never grow up into *them*, never get at all human –
which is being the wrong way up in a body once yours:
torment worse than the cranefly's, haggling over a corner
until he finds the sky, opens out like a strange
tasselled parachute and floats himself, dying,
into mountains grassy and sleepy as last week's childhood.

Pietàs

You were my sweetheart. Can I say so, now
I'm almost old, with no further claim to gender:
Now desire is a word and has no pulse
Beyond its own faint sigh, and love speaks simple prose?

You know how the crayoned collars we put on the spinning-tops
Made colour different? So, if I tell you my body
Remembers you, that's how: in delicate pastel strands
That will never be teased out while the top keeps spinning.

The girl closed like the man, the man soft as the child –
Such ironies of touch are bound to upset our curators.
Sweetheart, my first love poems should have been yours,
But to dare to break the glass has taken so many years.

I made myself a dress of stiff-collared lies
And the wind blew us both away. Only now can I return
Like a stream of tears over the stones of my wedding
To where you wait, a man my age, not yet

Dismissed, because I've handed you my camera,
And perch in front of you in my quaint ruched swimsuit.
One knee bent, school-grubby hands on hips,
I twitch my lips at the light, and think *beauty queen*.

Failed curls, limp breasts, no waist – and I'm trembling, because
I'm seventeen and everything's possible.
Then, in an after-flash, I see my flesh unchosen.
Your eyes tell me I'm lovely, so nobody else's can.

I found, of course, the usual steely wings;
Left you among flowerbeds, transplanting small fierce thirsts.
Sweetheart, the dead are rewarded: the children learn
It is only next door where the ruined parents go.

Against Posterity

Gather round me now, you older poets –
Poets in your late forties, early fifties,
Mid-fifties – you who understand
The significance of these small demarcations:
Poets of three-score years and pension book,
Superbly unretiring, with or without a *festschrift*
Made by the admirers you'll never become:
Poets triumphant in your racy seventies,
And you, especially you, in your eighties and nineties,
Maire, Dasenka, Kathleen – marvellous sisterhood –
Bring your short breath and your dancing stanzas.
And don't be shy, you grandfathers and great-grandfathers,
Though poems may be your only progeny –
Hey, you with the tinsel beard, no bardish pride!
This is a call for solidarity
Surpassing miserly gender (oh, forget about gender:
By now it's surely forgotten about us).
Spread the news of your brilliant forthcoming collection,
The Whitbread and the Forward in the bag,
But raise a not unkindly eyebrow at
The Gregory girls and boys still trembling at first base.
Tell us your publishers love you more and more,
But if you've travelled the hard road from nowhere
To sunny fame then down to the council tip
Of the out-of-date, declare with modest humour
The world has yet to match your three-legged stride
Along the crest of that hill it hasn't noticed yet.
Be tacit, but imply you won't go gentle
Like clowning Dylan, nor in Plath's hard rage,
To freeze with those who would have graced our gathering
With wit and beauty and magnificence
Had they cherished themselves as they cherished language.
Poetry's for grownups. So gather round, who know
Their music isn't the new rock 'n' roll
But a late quartet that sometimes bursts out laughing.
Bring your sustaining harmonies, let rip with your solos,
Unfurl surprises till the final chord,
When we'll forgive your silence – as ours will be forgiven -
And make way a little grudgingly
For the new recruits, who'll seem a shade too youthful.

Pledge to the Freight Canvasser

I'll take you with me when I board the ship
And if the ship turns out to be a boat,
The boat, a raft, the raft, a tattering branch
Flung from a boy's seaside story, tethered
At once to every whim that shakes the rootless ocean,
I'll stow your name, I'll roll it tinier than
Your shyest signature, and we'll be snug,
Low in the water, singing as we have to,
As ever targeted and separated
Children of the war. With hands and knees
Wrapped tight around our names, we'll sail together
Until the ocean tires and there's an orchard:
And if the orchard's just a single fruit-tree
And if the fruit tree is a single branch,
And if the branch has only one good blossom
It will be yours, to form you always, when
I leave your name, there, warrior, underneath your ship.

Anything/Nothing

He becomes lame
  she stops
    climbing mountains

he loses some of his hearing
  she loses
    some of her tongue

he forgets to admire her body
  she ceases to admire
    any body

young marriage doubles the joy
  old marriage halves it

  and so she begins
paring lengths from his sight

  but remembers to shout
a joke in his best ear
clink of glasses

  they share the mountain
at the kitchen window
determined to savour

  seagull, sheep, stone
he names the snowdrifts for her
the half-measure

  oh how they work to keep
this earth that's so much harder
so much bigger, now,

        than anything
        than nothing

To the Shipbuilder, his Tabernacle

Leave the shed-door open:
It's all that lights the garden once we've crossed
Your solstice-shaded birthday.
Dusty martyrs' crowns on the young ivy
Are the best we can do for autumn flowers:
Our rooftop-transept banishes the sunbeds
To Evensong by four.
But this door has a forest's eyes; when cedar
Bristles back to its origins, the day
Sticks like honey, never wants to let go.

Did we know we were buying sunlight,
Driving out to one of those desolate
Life-style hangers on the edge of town,
Strolling the wooden shtetl?
It was your birthday. I was feeling rich.
As if I'd been stockpiling English dreams
For the first Ukrainian-Jewish-Russian-Finn
Who'd crossed the border into B and Q.
I wrote a cheque to make the best and dearest
More yours than Moscow.

You got inside at once, opening crystals
Of space with a submariner's
Eye for horizons, deep in stacking-systems.
Tools lined the decks like sailors,
Some bright, some sleepy. Rusty captains stowed
Their wooden legs upright. Tins on tins,
Labelled *almond cake, pitted olives, ikra*
Rattled with machine-food.
You pinched the nameplate from your office door
When they 'retired' you, fixed it to the shed.

And if the wood by now
Is being turned by micro-organisms,
Glued with a frost of cobwebs,
The gentle molecules of oil and creosote
Tired of stretching: if I submit and say
That autumn's pollen, halo-ing the ivy,

Was gold enough, more than we could have asked for,
Don't go before I've told you, with a wife's sad humour –
Leave the shed door open
So that I'll sometimes see you.

Wood Lovers

And a time will come when we drive on, ignoring
The grassy welcome-mat outside the pine trees' barracks
And our infallible instinct to surprise
Some tiny village, light-forgotten, stained
Cupolas lined with pleated pearl and coral.
And a time will come when our legs refuse to vanish
Far enough to uncloud the bluebell islands,
Or the windflower archipelago, white as Sweden:
And then a time when there's no wood, no forest,
No signposts for the words that keep on saying your voice:
Gribochki, kolokolchiki, choroshi less.

gribochki, kolokolchiki, choroshi less: transliterations from the Russian for
mushrooms, bluebells (diminutive forms), *a good forest*.

Refresher Course

Drifting at dawn out of staticky hurricane dreams
to the clearest blue ever sieved through a wet tent wall,
to the shock of grass in its first-day sky, and the roar
of the river-beast, the whole sheep orchestra
sending each other a wobbly, hopeful 'A'
and never needing to reach the symphony,
we knew we had altered time. Time was our child
like the child of old parents, a huge reach
encompassed: we would shed years every day.

In or out of the tent, time flew: we caught it
occasionally, we gave it different nicknames,
to do with light. The only tune it knew
was *Variations of a Theme of Rain*:
gas-rings and rain, dishes and soap and rain,
blankets beginning to steam and sparkle; rain,
wood-fires spitting at rain, wine with a spritz of rain:
rain in the bones, pricking, darning, tugging.
Once, playing *Hunt the Sun*, it let us win:
we stood at the wet kissing-gate and felt
the brush of dim warm animals called rainbow.

Imagine a life as just-made glass, so clean
it was invisible, self-polishing.
It never asked us to notice it until
the leaving day. Stroke after stroke appeared
and wrote: *we were happy here.* And happiness paid
its last pound-coin to the casual farmer.
Our feet crept home as shoes, our wrists as sodden
watch-strap; we could see the day was filthy,
and time, drumming enormous adult heels,
hated our straw house, our joke umbrellas.
We talked about going back, perhaps next week.
But only one of us did. And only like this.

Swedish Exchange

When we entered the room it was white. The lampshade was blue, circular, patterned with circular holes. A white half-curtain at the window was printed with ellipses of different colours. There was a flat mirror in a wooden frame that was curved, lending the glass a faint concavity. A whitewood table and two chairs. A red mat.

We made the red mat dirty. On the table we put a glass of lilies-of-the-valley: they had cost thirty kroner on a street corner somewhere near the Klara church. The woman who sold them said: you must give them cold water! There is a blue dictionary on the table containing 30,000 *ord och fraser* and, on the window-sill, a lime-green tennis-ball containing a finite but unknown number of bounces. The mirror is full of badly hung clothes. Light sometimes leaks from the lampshade holes, the chairs refuse to sit at the table.

To make the room simple again we will have to leave it. We ourselves will have to re-complicate. This is a pity. We'd like to leave the room not as we found it but as we made it, impressed with our favourite transfers. The room would be grateful. And we would be white, clean, with natural wood features and a few splashes of primary colour, an excellent design for the modern human. We would close the door and not invite ourselves back in.

Portrait of God as a Creative Writing Student

Such a long Sunday
in March: north wind
mouthing my letter-box,
edging its way
into the bright room
where I calmly read,
having discovered this morning
that God exists
and has made the world
much as a first-year student
makes a poem – from himself
and any available language,
with many slides and hitches
and hopes and misconceptions
about what the hell it all is.

I see my duty clear:
to foster his self-esteem
and his humility
in equal proportions.
He must learn how to listen.
He must get used to revising.
So when I climb
the thin blue tree
of my dying brain, in a chill
brilliance much like this
March day, I will tell him
some of his ideas were good,
lots of his images
I liked – for instance, grass.
I'll show him what I'd cut out –
the adverbs and adjectives
that smelt of rot, and the rhymes –
their loud self-mockery.
God will be grateful.
I know his next world
will be an improvement
if not quite Shakespeare.
I look forward to reading it.

Quotations

What I like about quotations
Is their loneliness

What I like about loneliness
Is seven and a half vodkas-and-blackcurrant

What I like about blackcurrants
Are the sharp little stones inside their burst cushions

What I like about cushions
Is their lack of backbone

What I like about the backbone
Is its perfection

What I like about perfection
Is academic

What I like about academics
Is the way they curl two fingers when citing quotations

(Etc.)

A Word I Used to Know

Lincrustra? (Link Ruster? Lynn Cruster?)
'40s brand-name? Pronunciation disaster?
    That it meant anaglypta
I've lately deduced, but deduction wasn't an issue
Before I could spell, when words were to squeeze or to chew,
    Or smelt of some picture.

Lincrustra: it was a playground of dancing, identical
Roses, each in its own ring, with a diamondy spandrel
    Delightful between:
A child-high façade, nose-tip-friendly, that graced a fair portion
Of rooms in our tall end-of-terrace – some gloss, some emulsion,
    'Light Oak' or 'Nile Green.'

I'd read the Braille thoughtfully now, as a period detail,
A saleable feature: but that's not the reason, lincrustra,
I stroke you – my grandmother's pride, cherished weekly with Dettol
And Min-Cream, and, daily, for peak lower-middle-class lustre,
    Her soft yellow duster!

The Omen Bird

She flew onto the fence of every yard
And garden of our youth and raised, thrush-throated,
Her rueful, mothering, mournful little cry:
True love, true love, it's not true love, admit it.
You'll never have true, true love like Dad and I.

Why think about it now? Leave her to fly
The winds or nest where memories are more sheltered,
More sheltering. If he and I wrong-footed
The sex-dance, still its tune was in our blood
And it was rock 'n' roll, not some old lie:
True love, true love, it's not true love, admit it.
You'll never have true, true love like Dad and I.

And if one dawn I walked out of his garden,
Through mud and broken, lifeless stalks, the dream
That lured me was an orchard of my own.
Lark-song was not more distant than that scream:
True love, true love, it's not true love, admit it.
You'll never have true, true love like Dad and I.

It's years now since we loved and since we hated.
I'm dead to him. The orchard's down. So why,
Why does she perch on winter's crumbless ledge,
Her head alert, blinking a bright tin eye,
Almost as if she saw our old pine bed
Still held the slumped conundrum, loosely knotted,
And she was trying to lure us to the edge:
True love, true love, it's not true love, admit it.
I'd never be surprised if you two parted.

The Tour

It was the Irishwoman's Auschwitz.
Her shoes whispered over the frail unlucky spades
slapped to the paths by the self-cursing poplars,
printed an ooze on the breathless linos: *you are doing this
to me, Englishwoman.* From room to room, worst to
worse, we stirred the unprocessed grains of murder
till different crowns of ash lit up the rival
colours of our identically dyed red hair.
In a last new graveyard, elegy
tried to take our hands, show us the way through
by lettered light, the faintly carved
relief-work of Babel. Had there been one prayer-language
only – say, immaculate pagan Latin,
or masked, tender Yiddish, we could have closed our eyes,
but she saw the whole of Europe signatory
to the old Sassenach crime, the ghastly omission,
and I bit my fist like a pale East German schoolkid
chewing the dirt and skin in *Nazi*, swapping
stars with himself, as she keened the severed tongue.

The ghosts pressed back against the walls,
trying not to feed the present indignation,
straining not to be swallowed, not to become Israel.

The Polio Cup

You couldn't catch their germs. There was no risk.
Some couldn't move. *Poor things.* The luckiest maybe
Lurched on crutches, each strapped leg a cage.
They cried to go outside, so they were set
In iron chairs and beds, facing the sun.
You waved to them from the bus queue. Some waved back

And you, fazed by the etiquette, waved back
So they waved back and you were trapped, at risk
From seeming soft or cruel as iron. The sun
Pinched your eyes, your arm weakened. Maybe
Nurse would march out soon and issue sunset
And roll the children back and lock the cage.

The bus rolled up, opened its friendly cage.
Your wave was strong, final. You turned your back.
Now you could show that in your cagey twinset
There was a tough kid who took the risk –
A tough kid going somewhere brilliant, maybe
The pool with its splashes, shrieks, delirious sun.

In fact, you went to the park. You walked in the sun –
Mummy, Daddy, Carol-Ann – a cage
With three gold bars. You rattled them gently. Maybe
One fine day...? You kicked gravel, dropped back
Then raced ahead, to be at your own risk.
You watched the tennis, half a brown-limbed set;

A bowlsman barked 'Good wood, sir.' How you'd set
The world to rights if you could rule the sun
And air: children would breathe and never risk
Losing their dreams to the grown-ups' jealous cage.
You swung from trees till your rulers called you back.
You asked for an ice. They looked uneasy. *Maybe.*

Now you were ready to run away and maybe
Join that clamouring gang of 'riff-raff', set
On a go at the drinking fountain, splashing back
And forth the chained cup with the slice of sun
In its mouth. You'd grab it, swig from the leaky cage
Of germs, and live! Oh run, just run the risk,

The risk of life's sour tin, filled mouth, sweet *maybe*.
Your heart's an aching cage. You lost the sun.
Your muscles set. A childhood never grows back.

Mothers/Daughters

Like natives of a country
who know nothing of that country,
we planted houses which shuddered,
pumped oily outflow
into fresh water, stole each other's air —
and we told each other it was them,
the men, who'd ruined our land.

Learner

She tried to make a life out of dead things:
A woman's gravestone eyes, a man's drowned smile.
With all her breath, muscle, cherishings,
She tried to make a life. Out of dead things
False life alone can come, but since 'hope springs'
Et cetera, for a long laborious while
She tried to make a life out of dead things.

A woman's gravestone eyes a man's drowned smile.

Letter

(i.m. Yehuda Amichai)

Love is not, you told us, the last room
In the long corridor that has no end.
Young till that moment, I had not imagined
Rooms beyond love – not rooms with life in them,
But now I felt a season of decorum
Cooling my breeze. I thought I too could rise,
Brush off my suitors, seek those ghostly floors
Most distant from the heart and the heart's heat.
Reaching at last the *sanctum sanctorum*,
I'd notice further doors, hemmed with faint rays
(The corridor was long, you said, was endless),
Find rooms it seemed too soon to talk about
While time could laugh. Clutching your groundplan, still
Convinced, I came of age. And here I've learned
That the heart's room, as well, may have no end.
Windows may seal and fade, and doors unhandle,
Lit outlines melting into wall-thick mist.
Wherever you are now, in rooms beyond
My grasp, I write to say – it would appear
That the first room, love's, may also be the last
Though love is now an absence, cornered there.

The Fitting Room

I was a legend in my mother's lifetime
And marvelled as the name I never took
Did cute or comic things in simple rhyme
Or dazzled like an easy-reading book.
'But I grew up,' I said. 'What happened after?'
She didn't know. Perhaps her heart intoned,
'They are not long, the weeping and the laughter,'
But, terrified to entertain such thoughts,
She went on joining up the dot-to-dots,
And, at her side, the child of fifty groaned.

I had no life to share, few words to say,
Till she lay dying. Then, the legend spoke,
Spoke legends in the colours she'd have chosen,
I hoped, to warm a cave untouched by day.
Words failed her, but her mouth, crookedly open,
Seemed to be laughing at the little joke
Death makes of life. Since then, I've found a tongue
Too quick, I think, at argument and blame,
And yet I've half a hope she sits among
My readers – those who know my grown-up name.

She'll tell the tale that fits like me like a glove
And I won't feel diminished, saying Mother,
Mummy, Mum. Why is so much of love
The kind of gift you know was made by hand
And not made well, some weird, tenderly-knit
Garment that doesn't suit, won't ever fit?
I'll guess it was her love I called a legend.
I thought it shrank me, sought an ampler space.
But she's the legend now – the way I tell her,
My funny gift. My loss. My crooked face.

Autumn Colours

High over Petersburg, gold and red
Like a Khokhloma soup-spoon, a kitchen gleams
And mists with fragrance, just as it did
When you were the boy with the bowl of dreams.
But the grown-ups died and the tall young man
With the lacquered money and laughing wife,
Can't be the one who fills the word, *son*:
As he shakes your hand he unmakes your life,
    Saying 'Pack up your troubles, Pa, let's go
    To the Fountain of Youth or some place you know.
    The fountain's fucked and the weeds smell vile
    But the fags are cheap, so smile, boys, smile.'

And you picture the banners, red and gold,
And all they meant or should have meant:
They've gone with the gods and the country, sold
For a song whose words aren't any you learnt
As a Young Pioneer. You can move as you please
But the town on your papers isn't your town.
Each rolling Mercedes is full of old faces –
Same apparatchik, faster gun.
    Then pick up your kit, that place is scary.
    Better retire to Tipperary.
    It's a long long way, as the war-vets sing
    But nearer, my love, than your Leningrad spring.

Rogue Translations

1 *Once*
(*After 'Ya Vas Liubil' by* ALEXANDER PUSHKIN)

I loved you once. D'you hear a small *'I love you'*
    Each time we're forced to meet? Don't groan, don't hide!
A damaged tree can live without a bud:
    No one need break the branches and uncover
The green that should have danced, dying inside.
    I loved you, knowing I'd never be your lover.
And now? I wish you summers of leaf-shine
    And leaf-shade, and a face in dreams above you,
    As tender and as innocent as mine.

2 *Special Exhibition*
(*After 'Mirskaya Vlast' by* ALEXANDER PUSHKIN)

A craftsman made an image of a crucified god.
His prayer, in time, became a work of art
And stood in a museum under armed guard.
2000 years ago, the original prophet,
A mystery to us now, hung slowly dying,
Dying, as he'd lived, among the undeserving poor,
Flanked by thieves, his cherished women crying –
One said to be a virgin, one, a whore.
Now, where they leant, impassive policemen reign,
And no one else gets near the exhibit.
The celebs eye each other, sip champagne.
Christ isn't here. He couldn't afford the ticket.

3 *We'll Meet Again*

(After 'V Peterburge mie soidyomsya snova' by OSIP MANDELSHTAM.
The speaker is a South Londoner of the early 1940s.)

We'll meet again in 'Peter'.
We'll dig up that Victory sun
and say the word again –
our blessed, daft little word.
The Soviet night's a nag called Black Velvet.
The empty universe is a pint of Black Velvet.
We'll bet on the empty universe.
Long as our favourites are on-stage, our troupers
who never say die – long as you never say die, girls –
we'll all come up roses.

Like a cornered moggie, the town
whips up a humpback bridge complete with sentry.
A wicked car rips solo through the gloom –
cuckoo, cuckoo.
I don't need your old pass, ta very muchly.
You can tell the guard where to get off.
Give me crimson velvet, a couple of tickets,
that hush, that nervous rustling,
silky as silk stockings.
A girl cries 'whoops' and Venus takes a bow,
up to her cherries in roses.
I'm praying to you, little word. My daft little wonderful word.

Boredom stares at the gas-fire, roasting its knees.
Was that the sandman passing,
leaving a smear of ash
on the arms we knew and blessed?

Those crimson curtains, deep as orchestras,
Those treasure-boxes, stuffed
like gran's chiffonier
with clockwork captains and their china dolls –
bastards and hypocrites haven't got an inkling!
Put out the candles, son, if that's the boss's orders.
Put up the old black cretonne. The women'll just shrug
their luscious shoulders, won't you, girls, and keep
right on singing. Bless you.

Singing shoulders, blooming banks of roses,
the sun lit up all night – and you never saw sweet FA!

4 *The Grape-Picker*
(After Fasti, III. Non. 5th, by OVID*)*

By the fifth morning, when the dew has dried
    On the saffron cheek of Tithonus' wife, Aurora,
Instead of the Great Bear and the sleepy Herdsman,
    You'll see the Grape-Picker, curly-haired Ampelus,
Stretch out his boyish hand. This is his story:
    Child of nymph and satyr, he was playing
Among the Ismanian hills one day when Bacchus,
    Idly watching, fell for him utterly.
And he sang up a drunken gift, an enormous vine, fruit-laden,
    And trailed it over the highest bow of an elm tree.
Scrambling along to reach the glowing clusters,
    Ampelus lost his balance, pitched over headfirst.
Bacchus lifted the small corpse from the hillside.
    He placed it in a canopy of swaying, grape-bright stars.

5 *The Things He Liked*
(*After 'On liubil tri veshi na sveti' by* ANNA AKHMATOVA)

He liked secret agents, submarines.
He had a soft spot for the Thames Barrier.
And he was tied to me.

He read big books from remainder shops,
All about *things*, the things
He liked: secret agents, submarines,

Our Mysterious Universe,
The Volvo 300 Series,
And he was tied to me

Who couldn't read a fuel-gauge.
He hated long talks about feelings.
He liked secret agents. Submarines

Were a primitive fascination.
They were his youth, his memory,
And he was tied. To me

He was Naval Intelligence. I kept bugging him.
I stroked his prow, promised to play at whatever
He liked: *secret agents, submarines,*
And he was tied to me.

Genesis: The True Story

And Lo, the badness started on day one.
I parted blackwhite, landsea. Snake unhooked,
And took his slice, and drank the midday sun.

When I invented mating (good clean fun)
He thought up meat – the raw, the rare, the cooked
And Lo, the badness started. From day one,

We lived on others' lives. The way we've spun
That food-chain, there's no little link not hooked,
Taking its slice, drinking the midday sun.

I said *thou shalt not kill*. He cocked his gun.
I didn't even want to look. He looked
And loved the badness started on day one.

Beg pardon, world. Beg pardon for each son
I warmed and fed with war, for ever spooked
To take his slice, piss out the midday sun.

I'd rip the script, I would – re-write or run.
But all you impressarios scream, *You're booked.*
LOL@ your badness! Do it like day one.
Give us our slice. Bugger the midday sun!

To the Future Generations

Sweeties, you can't all be carried.
Though you're almost as light as sperm,
you're almost as numerous
and we've only got two pairs of hands
as mother used to say.

Darlings, you can't all have names:
we've got hearts, we've got favourites.
Some of you are top of our pops;
a few are on the tips of our tongues,
but some (that's life) are not.

Ladies and gents, please wait your turn.
It's no use waving and screaming.
You're not the only ones:
we're making more babies each minute
and the body-count's gonna be fantastic.
We've only got heads on our shoulders.

When Midnight's an Hour Away: A Pastiche

Young death-love. Count on it
For about as long as the well-fed average woman
    Ekes out her golden eggs –
Say, four to five decades to dance
With the roses & snow, the archaic flourishes
And edgy wee verbs ('this world I do renounce')
That became your whole aesthetic –
    Your moral, even – sense of
The passionate truth, the truest part of passion.
    Strong jazz. But didn't you play it?

    Whenever cruel appetite groaned
And language failed (your umpteenth mating ode
    Returned unread – just imagine!)
You'd watch yourself peel off the glue-
Kissed ribbon and slowly the contact-lens-thin, rose-tinted
Folds of your wrapping would follow, and there
Was the glittering red, the immortal just-what-you-wanted!
    It was all yours, if you dared.
It had always been yours, with your name on.
    And being so sure you waited.

    Oh, you had a future!
But just as there has to be last year's nest
    And yesterday's species,
There's an end to the pretty word, *oneday*.
You get to the bit where the small slow hours set aside
    For the act of despair
Spring open and, hard as a heart-beat, the notion
    Occurs that *to cease upon*
    The midnight is just what you don't
Fancy just yet. When the beautiful decades are done
And the fire as close as the comb to the ghost in your hair,
    What have you got to die for?

Rich Rhymes for Stroking Poor Pets

Skin I no longer stroke – not even in my mind.
That the biped's nomansland of it is mined,
Sank in at last: my thought-trails halt and turn there.
Rocks promise kinder holds, are guaranteed to turn their
Beautifully other cheeks. Among the mammals, I prefer
The flared-ear ones with flat-pack claws, savannah-coded fur.
Their teeth are shiny, though their breath is rank;
They strike with surgical precision over rank
And territory, but rarely kill their kind.
Their cupboard love's unfeigned. Yet sometimes they seem kind,
And nudge you when you say 'my pussikin'.
You feed them lies. They honour you as kin.
Oh, mouse-diviners, moonlight shiners, leaping sybarites,
Neat saboteurs of seed-drills, cyber rites,
Don't sniff my hand in case you hear the savings grow less,
But wrap your faces in your tails and smile, sublimely growlless.

Crazy Jane's Latest Ballad

I went along to the public ward,
    As a visitor I went,
And there was a monkey on a bed,
    With a drip and an oxygen tent.

I thought his grin was the grin of a skull
    But he could still grind air,
And the song he wrung from his squeeze-box lung
    Was called 'If you haven't been there'.

'If you haven't been there, don't talk about shame,
    Don't cry for the powers you've lost.
If you haven't just spent your body's last cent
    You know sod all about cost.'

Then I went along to the old folks' home,
    As a visitor I went,
And there was a witch with limbs like sticks,
    Her head to her stick-knees bent.

But she crooked her neck to peer at me
    And she sang though her gums were bare
And I heard through her gums and her bubbling scum
    'Girl, you ain't been there.'

'If you ain't been there, don't talk about shame
    Don't cry for the looks you've lost.
Till the buggers rob your brain's last bob
    You'll know sod all about cost.'

Then back I went to my little life,
    As a visitor I went.
I sniffed at the sky and I smelled its lie,
    And, God, it was a welcoming scent.

And I thought about fresh sweet skin, caved in,
    And a heart too scarred to care,
And I started to rumba to an old blues number,
    'Seems like I been there.'

'So roll me down to Rio, daddy,
    I'm the babe to splurge on.
Gimme collagen tits and transplanted wits
    And a struck off fertility surgeon.

'I'll love my pain with a morphine grain,
    I'll buy me the kisses I've lost.
My body's last cent will be saved, not spent –
    I know what my pride will cost.'

Letters Back

1

Dear Muse, my female first (apart from Sitwell
Who charmed me hugely at the age of eight),
Whose poems I re-hashed like Holy Writ, till
I learned to honour, not to imitate,
Forgive this impudence. I'm not pretending
Your spirit spoke, dictating me your choice
Of addressees. It's awfully English, sending
Tirades by post. You'd never use this voice
I've wished on you: compared to yours, it's tame.
You're 'Sylvia Plath,' you're almost my invention,
A thing of words. And all words cloud your name.
Yet fiction sometimes has a pure intention:
The thread of truth I chase and lure by ruse
I hope is yours. But the words are mine. Sing, Muse.

2

Dear Carol, I'm inclined to think you're bats.
But then I hear you've lately moved to Wales
And teach Creative Writing and keep cats:
Sorry to take the wind out of your sails –
Or should I spell that 'sales'? I do suspect
You're playing up, here, to the 'poetry scene,'
Auditioning for a bit-part in my act,
The movie, even? Still, I know you're keen
(Who's Sitwell, by the way?) and fairly pissed
At critics and biographers and *men*.
(What's wrong with men?) OK, if you insist,
Take up your quill. Don't bother me again:
I'm dead. Just try to get the scansion right.
And don't come on all tragic. Keep it light.

3 *To the Critics who Judged me a Fake*

You customs-men exclaim and seize my *Letters*
Home. 'She's schizo.' 'Where's her attitude?'
But, guys, that's how it used to be. Our betters
Demanded both success and gratitude.
A daughter knew her mother's sacrifice
In every twitchy nerve. The least she owed
Was sugar, spice and all things nice as nice.
Not the truth. Jesus! Not the poetry toad.
Twice immigrant, we'd shrink and shrink to fit
First the glass slipper, then the slippery ring –
Mum's own arena – where they hose the shit
And keep the clowns from smashing everything:
Where any talent not a social grace
Is contraband, or dirt: stuff out of place.

4 *To the Amateur Freudians*

Oh please! D'you really think my road was down
To Dadsville that sad morning. *Dad?* Who he?
My prey was live and kicking. Object one:
To drag the schlemiel back, back, back to me.
And, two: if nearly dying didn't spark
The spell, to die for real and fix his hash.
I wanted him to cry, the little jerk.
Jezebel, too. I wanted them to crash.
Not nice, I know. Of course, what bright wives *should*
Do is give their genius-hubbies rope
And turn a blind eye while the money's good.
No, it ain't me, babe. Love was still my hope
That morning when I knelt in stink and grease
To tug his heart undone, whisper Oh please...

5 *To the Queen of England*

Men slaughter harmless mammals, act the shaman,
Rap with ghosts, conjure with goddesses,
And who in your establishment would blame them?
Then, if they're ripping off babes' bodices
Instead of helping put their kids to bed,
Your knights will merely smirk – that's poet's licence.
And any way the wife was off her head.
You nod: those vulgar tears, that shocking violence.
It's so un-necessary, going ballistic...
A little infidelity's old hat
Among you royals, n'est-ce-pas? Re-do your lipstick
And heap the laurels on this diplomat-
Diplopic. But don't swallow all the charm.
His stuff about you's bollocks. (S'cuse me, Ma'am.)

6 *To a Rival*

Adrienne Cecile Rich, you weren't exciting!
Back then in sixty-two and sixty-three,
I was the one doing the red-hot writing.
And then you added DC to AC
And found a style I can't exactly praise.
Postmodern, is it? Well, your sense of form's
Kind of unbuttoned, on its holidays.
You reached the wreck, though, flippered up some storms,
Found the drowned face. The shore-bound shiverer died
Painfully, her lycra skin ripped off,
Trim craft in ribbons. No, not suicide
But huge divorce, long labour. *Mazel tov!*
The truth is yours. Women poets must dive –
Not flay themselves. Glad you came up alive.

7 *Another Entry for a Revised Mythology*

Meet Mr Arachne of the Guild
Minerva founded, weaving the long tale
In twice-dyed threads: our psychic battle-field.
A lurid web of horror and betrayal,
It fills the museum mind of hoi polloi,
His cloak-and-dagger version, starring Daddy,
The Daughter and the Prince who must destroy
The Dad – who's dead, but still a real baddie.
This scene shows the dénouement of the plot:
The father hides behind the boy whose skinny
English chest the girl zooms through like shot.
So Dad gets girl and Hero feels a ninny.
This story's not original, nor proven.
Spiderman's threads are mine, wildly re-woven.

8 *To a Young Narcissus*

What are the lyric poet's proper themes?
Not 'self-discovery, self-definition?'
Not the 'Personal Helicon' and its streams
Where the drowned face shivers recognition?
Poet-Professor, literal and prescriptive,
The poet in you mars what you profess,
Versing his fields until they're fruitful, fictive
And dubious as 'self-forgetfulness'.
We warm the bones, arrange the stones again,
And it's our breath makes them extraordinary.
You knew this once, and carved it with your pen,
A mythic ploughboy in a mythic Derry:
Young poets sing themselves, themselves to hear.
And some, of course, stay young their whole career.

9 *To Mother*

Therapists and shrinks, amateur writers
All, made it come true, the Freudian gist
Of women's grief – a myth bound to delight us
College girls turned newly classicist.
I'm not denying my loss, the dad-shaped trauma,
Just claiming that the surgery went wrong.
After I saw the poem in it, the drama,
I pitched the story up and found my song.
Was I forced back or freed? I think I'd found
The balance, till the myth was darkened by
Re-telling, and got rooted in the ground
Of all my being, burnt into my sky.
It was one fable but I had another
Where you were loved and sought and mourned for, Mother.

10 *To a Playwright Collector of Buttons*

The saddest part of being fatherless –
You never learn to do the things men do
To save their souls; the way, from trash and mess,
They build their nerdy heaven. David, you
Are into buttons, tarnished eyes that stare
From walls and mouldings round your writing-den.
The cheap bright grins say, 'Anywhere but here,
Writing this bloody play!' I might have chosen
Stamps, but stamps meant letters, desperation
Of various kinds. My 'play' was tongue-and-groove
With work, no tiny holes for respiration,
A seamless miracle I wove and wove
From every thread that blew across my life.
In fact, there were no threads that 'blew across' my life...

11 *To Any Poet or Would-Be Poet*

...And that's what made me great! If love's mere part
Of life to man but 'woman's whole existence',
The same, I dare suggest, is true of art.
I courted poems, countering all resistance,
Till they were mine, my nerves, skin, hormones, breath.
They were the love, they were the death I chose.
With every year my corpse looks less like death
Because it's made of poems. And love. Who knows
How hard it might have been sustaining that.
What power has art to breed at menopause?
What form has passion when you're old and fat
And all you do together is the chores?
Those the gods love die young. Don't imitate
Me – or yourself. 'Bye now. I've got a date.

The Turnstile

How long ago, was it, we lived near the Rhine
in that apartment-block above the music shop
with the minimalist window and snappy turnstile,
and you worked a ten-hour day while I sketched beside the river,
sunbathed on hard white stones and thought about my children
from whom I'd stolen this – a second life, a life
with you? But you had been here before:
you had been here too many times before
And knew love came to conclusions I hadn't reached.

I looked along the fast-flowing river
and saw the open book, the signature
of a bridge, shadowy promises compressed
so heavily their darkness seemed prismatic.
You were younger than I am now.
I thought it was the beginning of the truth,
some pure, recovered destiny we'd launch out on.
At last, I've caught you up, caught on to the rhythm that says
there are no new starts outside the various fictions.
Our lives have one beginning: that is their shape.
We'll be on track, embedded, wherever we go next,
separating as we move through the turnstile.